The Story of Freyja, The Peregrine Falcon

Illustrations by the children of the York, Maine School System

Story by Calvin Healey, 2nd Grade,
assisted with data provided by the Center for Wildlife

Front cover illustration by Joshua Gennaro, 2nd grade

Back cover illustration by Hannah Mae Gennaro, 4th grade

Edited by Kate Headen Waddell

Graphics by Julie Garman, Pipedream Studio

The Story of Freyja, The Peregrine Falcon

Sophia Roe, 2nd Grade

Meet Freyja

Hi, my name is Freyja and I am a Peregrine Falcon.
I am named after Freyja, the Norse goddess of love and magic.

I live at the Center for Wildlife in York Maine, a cool place that helps animals like me.
This is the story of how I came to live there.

Amelia Vetter, 2nd Grade

I was born in Worcester, MA. It was kind of noisy but boy were there a lot of pigeons to feast on! We love pigeon pizza with fries... just kidding!

Can you find my nest? I'll give you a hint. It is on top of the big skyscraper.

This is my family. I'm the one to the right of my mom with the cool egg hat. On the far left are Joe and his twin sister Sally, both still in their eggs, sleeping away. Snooooore! Quiet down you two!

Joe Jr. is the one next to Sally, my Mom is the tall one, and finally, it is me, Freyja. The lone ranger on the far right is Betty Lou Who.

The Peregin Falcon can div up to 250 mph! They are the fastest animals on earth.

Gabe Sarno, 2nd Grade

Stuff I Bet You Didn't Know About Peregrine Falcons

If you are paying attention, you probably already guessed that a Peregrine Falcon is a type of bird (because of the feathers, eggs, and beak, silly!).

peregrines usua
have 3-5 babie
at a time

Hope McSherry, 2nd Grade

Peregrine moms normally have 3 to 5 babies at a time. Peregrine babies are hatched from eggs, which the mother bird lays in a nest.

Alea Galbadis, 2nd Grade

Before I was born, my mom made our nest out of straw, weeds, and soft feathers. She made it blend in so that bigger birds wouldn't find us while she was out finding food for us. My nest was soooo snuggly like a big down pillow with super fluff built in.

6

Laura Wilson & Zoe Lafleurklef, 3rd Grade

Check out my Mom's claws! They are hinged, sharp and strong. Claws of steel! Fancy people call them "talons."

Here's mom, clinging to a branch with her talons of steel. Her eyes are scanning for mice or other delicious creatures for lunch.

Ella Holland, 2nd Grade

That's what we eat. Mostly birds, some rodents, and even small mammals.

Here is my mom out there looking for a juicy pigeon for me and my siblings to eat. My mom was awesome at catching pigeons and other prey right out of the air... whammo!

Emma Catling, 2nd Grade

Take a look at our wings. A pretty snazzy shape eh? Almost like a boomerang, zip! My mom uses her wings to catch up with prey lickety-split!

Would you like to fly? Let me tell you how much fun flying is. We can soar through the sky like a lightning bolt along the tops of mountain peaks and over fields.

My favorite thing about flying is finding food. You have to be stealthy like James Bond to catch your prey in mid-flight.

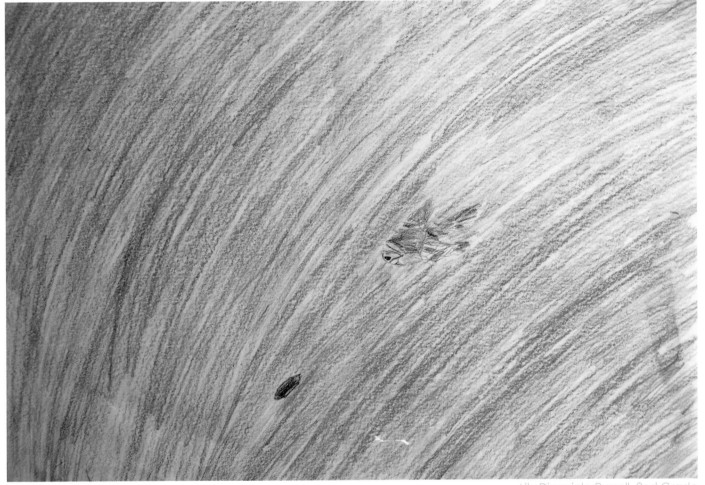

Want to hear something amazing? Peregrine Falcons can dive at speeds of up to 250 mph. We are the FASTEST animals on earth. Zipity zoom zoooom!

Cheetahs are slow pokes compared to us!

Here is a cool fact that most kids don't know. Peregrine Falcons are used at airports to scare away birds that could harm airplanes.

Did you know that birds can accidentally get caught in jet engines? These accidents kill the birds and can cause airplanes to crash.

Go Falcons! Way to keep those planes and birds safe!

Peregrine Falcons
live in fields!

Ella Abisi

Ella Abisi, 2nd Grade

How Peregrine Falcons Almost Became Extinct – and How We Saved Them!

Peregrine Falcons are still an endangered species where I'm from, but not across the whole country anymore. Do you know what endangered is?

Some kids think Barney is an endangered species because he is the only purple and green polka-dotted talking dinosaur on earth. I guess that is kind of right.

An endangered species is actually a living animal that is almost extinct. In other words, there aren't many left in the world.

In the 1970's, people started to notice that there weren't very many Peregrine Falcons around.

Scientists did some research. They found that chemicals like DDT (used to kill bugs on farm crops) were weakening the egg shells so the baby Falcons could not survive.

People learn from their mistakes and they get smarter. Because of smart scientists and people that cared about us, DDT was banned in 1972. But the Peregrine Falcons were still endangered.

We needed more help!

Aidan Martin, 2nd Grade

Dum dah daha dah…Tom Cade to the rescue! He worked at the Cornell Laboratory of Ornithology (that means people who study birds!) He founded the Peregrine Fund, which was dedicated to researching and saving the Peregrine Falcon. He's our hero!

Then the "Peregrine Project" was launched, and scientists, volunteers, bird lovers, wildlife rehabilitators, and others came together to breed Peregrine Falcons (like me!) in captivity and release them where they used to live before DDT was used.

It was pretty bad back in the 70s. In 1978 when we were put on the federal endangered species list there were only about two pairs of Peregrine Falcons left in the state of Maine and one in New Hampshire. Yikes!!

Thanks to the ban on DDT and the Peregrine project there are now over 23 breeding pairs of Peregrines in Maine. Way to go Maine!

In fact, we've rebounded all over the United States! Look at all of us up there! From 1972 to the early 1990s over 6,000 Peregrine Falcons were bred and released in over 37 states.

We've even been taken off the federal endangered species list! We're not totally out of the woods yet; Maine and New Hampshire decided to keep us on their state endangered species lists.

Cavan McNamara, 2nd Grade

People have learned that healthy wild birds ultimately mean healthy humans, and many people are using different ways to garden and farm other than chemicals.

Yeah, we should all be proud of our progress. Hoo rah!

But chemicals aren't our only danger...

Jay Gardoqui & Quenton Convery, 2nd Grade

Look Both Ways Before You Fly

Let me tell you how I almost became extinct.

I was born in 2004, and soon after that I left the nest for my first flight. That's called "fledging."

Yahoo, here I go!

Have you ever noticed all that yummy food that people throw out on the road as they're driving by? Well, mice sure do.

One day I zeroed in on a mouse munching on some delicious leftover human food – I think it was an apple or banana. I saw the car coming, but I don't really understand what cars are, so I kept flying right towards that mouse, thinking that the car was far enough away...

But whammo, it was going faster than I thought, and I got hit.

What can I say? It was my first time flying and I didn't know what a car was.

I crashed into the windshield and then I don't really remember much after that.

My friends at the Center for Wildlife tell me that a nice person found me knocked out and dizzy on the side of the road.

Greta Buttignol, 2nd Grade

Let's give it up for the person who helped me! Hoo rah, hoo rah!

Thankfully she was nice enough to use her cell phone and call for help.

Colleen Daly, 2nd Grade

Can you find the Red Cross on the building down in the forest? Come on you can find it?

That's Tufts Wildlife Clinic in Grafton, Massachusetts. After my accident, they were kind enough to keep me in a warm, safe and cozy place so I could get the medical help I needed. Did you know that animals need the same kind of medical stuff that people do? We sure do!

I lived at Tufts for awhile and once I got better they sent me to the Center for Wildlife in York, Maine.

It's a great place that helps all sorts of injured animals like me.

Once I got there, I had to get used to my environment and learn to trust my caregivers. They did a great job helping me to learn to use my flight enclosure to get healthy and strong.

They gave me ramps and ladders and all sorts of cool stuff so I could get around safely since I was disabled. My environment felt just like the wild – which I loved because we don't like to be treated like pets.

It is a nice place and I love having lots of friends like Zipper the corn snake and Edna the albino porcupine! Edna lives there because she is all white. Can you believe it? She is an all-white porcupine!

Jordan Liddy, 2nd Grade

Now that I am healthy I get to travel to schools and help educate and inspire children about wildlife and conservation.

Put your wings in! On three... one, two, three "Go Peregrine Falcons!"

Anthony Panteleos, 2nd Grade

What YOU Can Do to Keep Wildlife Like Freyja Safe

Wild animals shouldn't have to get hurt. Holy pigeons! What are you doing?

Don't throw food out the window. See that banana in the middle of the road? Fruit thrown out the window is the worst! Oh, and don't think you can just throw it super hard – it'll just bounce off a tree, and slide back into the road....

Charley Feugill, 2nd Grade

If you do find a wild animal that needs help, remember that it's nice to help wildlife that's been hurt, but it's also important to know what to do.

David Eftimov, 2nd Grade

You can't make wildlife your pet because it's dangerous for them and for you. And if you touch the wildlife you could get sick or make them sicker.

So, if wildlife is hurt you need ask a grown up to help you bring it to a place in your town like the Center for Wildlife.

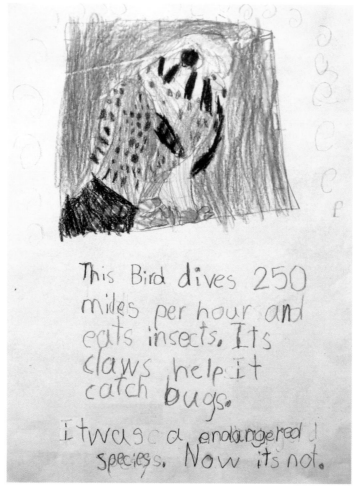

This Bird dives 250 miles per hour and eats insects. Its claws help It catch bugs.

it was a endangered species. Now its not.

Michael Gregory, 2nd Grade

Thanks for reading my story. We have learned so much from one another! Humans have really helped Peregrine Falcons and other wildlife species by reducing the use of pesticides and raising awareness.

You humans have learned from us and we have become a sensitive and accurate barometer (a cool way to measure!) of environmental health. Let's face it, we eat the same fish and drink the same water. So when you pay attention to our health, you keep healthy too!

Thank You!
We would like to thank 2nd grade teacher, Carrie Stearns, for spearheading the Freyja art contest; Kristen Lamb, Michelle Gorayeb, Susan Hansen, Karen McElmurry and all the rest of the Center for Wildlife staff, volunteers and interns; our veterinarian, Dr. John Means, for his medical attention to Freyja, and for teaching us how to work with a super-smart falcon; YeomanTechnologies.com and InnerCircleCommunities.com for their generous sponsorship of the editing and graphic design, and for their overall expertise to make this book happen; and to all the students at York, Maine elementary and middle schools who participated in the art contest. Special thanks to the members of the Seacoast Water Garden Club www.seacoastwatergarden.org for their ongoing support of CFW, and for helping to sponsor initial publishing of this book.

Reader's Art Contest: Have some fun and color Freyja, or draw your own illustration of Freyja on the next page. Then upload your art as a photo to the wall on the CFW Facebook page www.Facebook.com/CenterForWildlife to compete in our reader's art contest.

Peregrine Falcon Fun Facts

- Peregrines can dive at speeds of up to 250 mph and are the fastest animals on earth.

- Peregrines nest in a 'scrape' on the side of cliffs and have adapted to living on skyscrapers.

- Peregrines usually have 3-5 babies at a time.

- Peregrines' preferred prey are other birds that they catch in the air.

- Peregrines fledge from the nest at 5-6 weeks old. After practicing hunting with their families they are typically completely on their own at 8 weeks old.

- Peregrines that live around New Hampshire and Maine migrate to South America each year.

- Peregrines are used at airports to scare away birds that could harm airplanes.

- Some farmers sprayed crops with chemicals like DDT to fight broad range of insects.

- DDT stayed on leaves and entered watersheds during heavy use (1950s to 1970s) and was ingested by insects first, then made its way up the food chain to Peregrines and eagles.

- DDT did not allow Peregrines to uptake calcium, and when moms went to incubate their eggs they would crush them. Some Peregrines went a long time (10 years!) without having babies or adding to their populations.

- In 1970, Professor Tom Cade at the Cornell Laboratory of Ornithology founded the Peregrine Fund, dedicated to the research and re-establishment of the Peregrine Falcon. DDT was banned in 1972 as a result.

- In 1972 the "Peregrine Project" was launched and scientists, volunteers, bird enthusiasts, wildlife rehabilitators, and others came together to captively breed and release Peregrine Falcons to their original nesting sites. From 1972 to the early 1990s, over 6,000 Peregrine Falcons were bred and released in over 37 states.

- Peregrines were put on the federal endangered species list in 1978 in Maine, and there were only two pairs of Peregrine Falcons left in the state of Maine and one pair in New Hampshire.

- As a result of the ban on DDT and the Peregrine Project, there are now 23 breeding pairs of Peregrines in Maine. They have been federally delisted, but remain on the Maine and New Hampshire state endangered species lists.

Take our fun quiz to test your knowledge: www.tinyurl.com/TheStoryOfFreyja

About the Center for Wildlife in Cape Neddick, Maine

The Center for Wildlife is a private, non-profit organization whose mission is to rehabilitate and provide sanctuary for sick and injured wild animals, and to promote respect for wildlife and the environment.

Our mission also includes raising public awareness of the many wonderful wild species that live among us and a heightened sensitivity to the impacts humans have on their lives. Your purchase of this book helps us continue our work with wildlife and the community.

Learn more about Center for Wildlife and Peregrine Falcons:

▶ www.yorkcenterforwildlife.org

▶ www.wikipedia.org/wiki/Peregrine_Falcon

▶ www.Peregrine-foundation.ca/info/conservation.html

▶ www.birds.cornell.edu/Publications/LivingBird/summer99/missionaccomplished.html